RIDING HOME

HELEN POTREBENKO

TALONBOOKS   VANCOUVER   1995

Published with the assistance of the Canada Council

Talonbooks
201 - 1019 East Cordova
Vancouver, British Columbia
Canada V6A 1M8

Typeset in New Baskerville 11/13 and Optima and printed and bound in Canada by Hignell Printing Ltd.

First Printing: August, 1995

Acknowledgements: "The Drooping Rose" appeared in *TickleAce*; "The Hero of 1981" in *BC Literary Monthly*; "Job Interview" in *Room of One's Own*; "Riding Home" and "The Rules Nowadays" were printed as broadsheets by Lazara Press.

Canadian Cataloguing in Publication Data

Potrebenko, Helen, 1940-
    Riding home

    Poems.
    ISBN 0-88922-356-4

    I. Title.
PS8581.O76R52 1995   C811'.54   C95-910210-8
PR9199.3.P67R52   1995

To Maggie Benston
1937-1991

and all the others who provided assistance for some or any of the
poems in this book:

Earl Scott
Euphoniously Feminist & Non-Performing Quintet
Penny Goldsmith
Ruth Lea Taylor

...Love & Gratitude

RIDING HOME

I was riding home on the moped, singing;
throttle open, downhill, singing;
wearing a dress, riding home and singing,
when the motor stopped.

Mabel,
that's my moped,
stopped dead.
Sudden silence.
Geez.
Wouldn't start.
Tried
a dozen times,
maybe a hundred.
Hot day.
Sweat.

I was walking down Renfrew looking for a phone
to call my husband and there's a man yelling at
and shaking a woman. Took off my helmet,
wiped my glasses and sunglasses. Still there.

Yelling,
pushing,
crying.
Oh my.

Excuse me!
Yes, you!
Stop that!
Right now!

Then I say to the woman: can I help,
and she curls her lip and looks away

from this apparition in besweated pink dress
and blue helmet, leading a moped.

She sneered
at Mabel.
Curled her lip.
Said she was fine.

So I said to the man: keep your hands off her,
and he's sobbing: but she's always like this.
It's her right to be like this, I shouted,
not knowing in the least what "like this" was.

Never did find out.
It's her right.
Hope it's not
something bad
like drugs
though.

Well, I said, I only stopped because my moped broke.
And the man stopped crying in mid-sob,
wiped his face, walked over to the moped
and started tinkering with Mabel's spark plug.

It's true.
I was there.
Stopped in mid-sob.
Tried to fix the bike.

Mabel wouldn't fix; he started crying again.
I walked down Renfrew looking for a phone,
looking back to see he wasn't pushing or hitting—
told him not to even if she was like this.

Lotta people
like this;

some like that.
Can't hit 'em
about it
though.

I found a pay phone. Then up comes a muscle car,
out steps a tough in a tight T-shirt, with tattoos
and a tool kit. And while he's tinkering,
two more drive up. Same cars, same tattoos.

Haven't seen
so much muscle
since I left
the Pathology lab.

So when my husband gets there, there's
besweated me and a whole mess of muscles
monkeying with Mabel's manifold. He says
he's glad there's still Good Samaritans around.

And there are.
Hard
to recognize
sometimes.

AGING PARENTS

In olden days, I understand,
mothers blended into old age
in rocking chairs
with shawls,
like silvery, wrinkled angels
and then faded away
leaving behind the memory
of home-baked bread and sweet smiles.

But the mothers I meet sulk and whine
and yell at their grown children
in language shocking in one so old.
Instead of fading away,
they rage and denounce daughters,
who are themselves aging:
scream of betrayal and pain,
demand instant solutions
for the age-old problems of old age.

The mothers I meet in nursing homes
collect crackers and plastic jellies
and complain at visitors for not visiting hourly.
I have not seen them rocking or smiling
but rather,
rising in their beds and wheelchairs,
leaning on canes and walkers,
to curse aging daughters
for the world they never made,
offering them as solace,
wizened oranges,
dried crackers
and small plastic portions of imitation maple syrup.

A Poem for Douglas Glover, Steve McCaffery, All Language Poets, the Editorial Collective of *Paragraph* Magazine: For the Edification of Janie MacDermot

White man got no story to tell;
white man got no story to tell.
He got the power;
he got the privilege;
white man got no story to tell.

White man go: yaba yaba yaba goo goo goo;
white man go: gaba gaba gaba moo moo moo;
white man go: shriek, howl, doo, doo, doo;
and the Canada Council give him money
the University of New Brunswick give him money
and the University of Lethbridge give him money
and the University of Anywhere give him money
and the National Magazine Award give him money
and any provincial arts council give him money.
White man go: yowza, yowza, yowza, boo, boo, boo.

White man spit on moral fiction;
white man don't need moral;
white man spit on story;
white man got no story to tell.

Kurdish women have a story to tell:
there is no one to listen.
Ethiopian mothers have a story to tell:
nobody cares.
Some Canadians making land claims
have a story to tell.
White man got the land
and no work to do;
he don't need to tell no story.

White man got no story to tell.
He has men of colour
and women of all colours
to do his work.
He don't want to tell the story.

White man go: shrill howl me me me;
white man go: power privilege me me me;
white man go: yowza yowza I I I;
white man go: money money money.

BAD FIRES BURNING

Workers have unions at some times in some places:
slave labour cannot produce
precision industrial goods.
Peasants are never allowed to bargain
because starving people can and do
produce food for industry.

Peasants will never voluntarily
give up their food.
They grow food and then wish to keep it
for their own use.
One solution is taxation
but peasants, on the whole,
prefer eating to paying taxes.
An army is required.
It works reasonably well in many countries.
The dirty little wars
are only mentioned in passing.
Nameless people
carrying on disgusting little wars.
But armies, too, must eat
and guns and bullets are expensive.

If peasants were paid for their produce,
they would sell it
in order to buy other food and goods,
but that's too expensive a solution
to the peasant problem.
There is no other way to build empires
except off the unpaid labour of peasants.

The partly voluntary drive of 1929-30
to put peasants on collective farms in the USSR
was not successful.

So in 31-32, it was done again,
done better.
The survivors all joined collectives.
So short a time to be free of serfdom!
Now again peasants may not leave the land
to which they are bound.
And now peasants no longer keep their produce
for their own use
and sell the surplus to the state.
Now the state owns all the produce
and if there is a surplus,
sells it to the peasants.
So after a day's labour for the state farm,
peasants can relax by doing another day's labour
the same day, in their own garden.
It's only labour
and even peasants consider their labour valueless.

But before that, they,
who rebelled every generation
against the serfdom of the tsars,
fought one more dirty little war.
They burned and pillaged and killed
their own belongings.
They ate all their animals.
They turned their grain into alcohol.
And they burned, burned, burned.
Bad fires burning
in an awesome winter's fire,
lighting the way to despair and death
and Siberian exile.
Not for them the choice of liberty or death
only the choice of slavery or death.

Long after the fact, the estimates are
of five million dead Ukrainians.
But how many others?

Different empires have different armies;
the American empire has money and can buy
local armies to enforce colonial famines.
Peasants die in El Salvador and Somalia,
as they died in Vietnam, Afghanistan,
as they died in the Soviet Union.
Some of them get to be a national resistance
rather than some scummy drunken burning
and maybe this is progressive
and maybe it isn't.

Peasants are, on the whole, illiterate
and, on the world's stage, voiceless.
The armies sent to take the food
also guard the schools and media.
So there were only the fires
burning in the long winter.
Bad fires burning
in the long winter nights.

The succeeding generations
are docile though sullen
and given to drunkenness.
They hoard no food.
Maybe they dream of fires
and maybe they don't.

August, 1987

BIKERIDER

After Janie got her new bike, she spent the rest of the summer riding up and down the alley. She wasn't allowed on the street and the park was only accessible by crossing a busy street so she was confined to the alley. Not that Janie thought of it as being confined: the alley was her world.

Ride, ride, ride, oh, bikerider, on your new and perfect bike, for the world is large and there is time enough and space enough for what you need to do.

Sometimes the boys were also riding their bikes and then Janie thought of them all as a thundering herd of buffalo, thundering across the plains. Although she had only the haziest notion of what plains looked like, she knew they wouldn't have speed bumps, nor would cars come zipping down every once in a while, but this did not bother her. It is no problem for a thundering herd of buffalo to separate slightly to make way for an obstacle as it hurtles by in its thundering thousands.

She knew all the adults in the alley but never spoke to them. In fact, she hardly ever spoke to anyone and when she did, they leaned over and asked her to speak up which Janie found embarrassing. She preferred her sister yelling at her to, for pete's sake, speak up, than the adults being kind.

She didn't have anything to say even had she been able to make herself heard. She wanted to be left alone to ride up and down the alley. She didn't want, for example, Old Slippylips hailing her. Old Slippylips proclaimed to the world her love of children and said hello to Janie every single time Janie rode by her back yard which was several hundred times a day. Although Janie developed an automatic nod and smile, that wasn't always satisfactory.

Suppose, for example, you were the sheriff about to catch the bad guy, would you pause long enough to nod and smile to Old Slippylips? And what about the space chase where the bad guys' space ships were firing laser beams only compuseconds behind you?

Ride for your life, oh bikerider, ride, ride like the wind, do not be impeded by some old lady working in her garden.

Sometimes Janie's sister's boyfriend, the one Janie thought of as Hardheaded Jim, teased Janie about her bike riding and once he rode his Harley chopper up and down the alley beside Janie on her bike, revving and belching smoke. Jokeyjoe and Boozebreath came out to gawk and laugh and Janie was humiliated. She couldn't even stop speaking to Hardheaded Jim since she never did speak to him.

Ride, ride, ride, oh bikerider, for the dogs of powerlessness snap at your heels.

Janie could not remember how she had spent summers before she got the new bike. Of course, she must have read but reading was like breathing and could not really be considered an activity. She couldn't ask anyone at home about it. Her mother and father were nearly always at work and when they got home, her mother would yell at Janie's sister for not having the housework done or dinner cooked. Janie's sister was too busy to do such things, being either occupied with going out with Hardheaded Jim or Sir Reginald or preparing to go out with one of them.

Janie's sister could rarely do housework because it was of consuming importance to have her nails just right. How could she dust if her nails weren't dry? And suppose, even if they were dry, some household activity caused them to get chipped? A chipped nail was an occasion for lamenting followed by gloomy preoccupation with repair of the ravaged nail. Then there was the matter of hair which took up incredible amounts of time and consideration.

Sometimes Janie took time out from riding her bike to follow her sister around. Her sister spent hours on her hair. She didn't really have time to talk although sometimes she would pause to yell at Janie for not talking. Then there was her face which had to be carefully studied from all possible angles and covered with varieties of goop.

Once in a while, Janie's sister would lecture Janie about the right way to look after one's hair, face and nails. Such instruction puzzled Janie since she had not yet decided if she wanted to be an adult. So she would escape from her sister's friendly instruction with much more eagerness than she ever fled her sister's wrath.

Ride, ride, ride, oh bikerider, on your new and perfect bike, fleeing the ravages of false expectations, riding to the wind in your hair, riding to the sunshine on your back, riding to the joy of life and motion.

Not until nearly the end of the summer did anything untoward occur.

Janie was riding, riding, riding. She had her head down and was pumping slowly because she was part of a gang of bikeriders pulling a riverboat on the Mississippi. Over there in the centre of the alley was the Mississippi River with the riverboat on it and over on both sides of the river were the toiling bikeriders, pulling the riverboat. On the riverboat were dressed up ladies with madeup faces, perfectly done hair and unchipped nails. The ladies were practising their songs and dances for the next stop the riverboat was to make, while the toiling bikeriders pulled the boat down the river.

Thus engaged, Janie did not see a car backing out of a driveway into the alley. The back fender of the car hooked the bike and knocked it down. Janie fell down behind the car, shaken and terrified. The car was still backing slowly and Janie found that she was looking at the tire treads of the right rear wheel as it slowly came towards her face.

Then she heard Old Slippylips screaming. She was screaming stop, stop, stop in a funny high-pitched voice, as Janie watched the tire coming towards her face. Then she heard Boozebreath. My, what a bellow that man had! And was that Fuzzface, running and hollering? She would have liked to see what Fuzzface looked like running and hollering but she was unable to tear her eyes away from that tire coming slowly towards her face.

The tire stopped. Someone pulled Janie out from under the bumper. Daffydilly jumped out of the car and came running around, breathing funny and gasping, oh my god, oh my god.

And Janie saw that she was the very centre of attention, that all the screaming and the running and the red faces and the funny way people were breathing, had to do with her. It was unbearably embarrassing and for a moment, she wished she'd been killed dead by the car.

Fuzzface picked up the bike and looked it over, checking the wheels and turning the pedals by hand. Then he shrugged and handed the bike to Janie. Everyone looked very happy and talked all at once. Janie wanted to get on her bike and ride away but it seemed impolite since everyone was patting her and exclaiming over the bike. So she stood around awkwardly, not in the least knowing how to behave.

I'll walk you home, Old Slippylips said finally.

At home, Janie's sister took time out from recreating her hair to thank Old Slippylips. Then she kept Janie inside for nearly an hour to do dishes and be scolded.

But finally Janie could go again and ride in the alley.

Ride, ride, ride, oh bikerider, for the bad wheel stopped; the good wheels ride. Time and life may be fleeting and fickle but there is time enough and space enough for what you need to do.

BRING TO ME

Bring to me your tattered papers,
your unreconciled bank statements from 1987,
your dusty boxes of crumpled receipts
and I will make a ledger of them.
Bring to me your unfiled and unanswered letters
with no date stamp or return address
and I will make them
correspondence.

When you see a drunk crawling down the street,
you can tell right away
he never kept a household ledger.
When you see a jogger, red-faced and panting,
you can instantly conclude
he doesn't keep proper books.
Reading the ads for the new age spiritual
capitalist rip-off,
you think: people wouldn't fall for this
if they always
did their bank reconciliation.

Religious people have to accept
things on faith, of course,
so they never check
the addition on financial statements
nor work for social change.
They have to accept
that someone knows better
and never discover
that the ultimate mysteries
like god and a statement of income and expenses
should be calculated
and questioned.

If people kept proper books
there would be no need for drugs,
or violence,
or delinquency, juvenile or otherwise.
The police would be kept only to rescue
treed kittens.

Bookkeeping is informative, orderly
and comforting.
There is no one too drugged,
too degraded
that they cannot find joy in a
ledger card.
No matter how depressed you are,
the adjusted balance on your bank statement
must equal
the balance in your cheque book.
No matter how unhappy a childhood you had,
debits always have to equal credits.

The ilk that includes racists, anti-Semites
and other unclean, evil-doing things,
seems unaware that their books
will be balanced by others,
eventually.

I'm not telling this to everyone,
just Sheila and selected women's groups.
The meaning of life is that
debits have to equal credits.
Or maybe
the meaning of life is that
the great goddess created plants
and we are here only
to breathe in oxygen
and breathe out carbon dioxide
for the benefit of plants.

Our duty is
to breathe and make compost
so debits will equal credits
as it were.

CENSORSHIP

Sex and violence cannot be censored;
this would be an infringement
of human rights,
free speech,
the rights of writers,
and the right to information.
Only women's issues are to be censored.
Books completely concerned
with, for example, day care,
do not get published.
They are not of literary merit,
or universal concern.

Universal concerns are:
a man catching a fish,
rape, torture, war
and other forms of barbarism.
Universal concerns do not include
any rights of children,
living with spousal violence,
or poverty.

Poverty finds its way
into literature
only to illustrate some other point
like, maybe, man's inhumanity,
the black inner depths of every man's soul,
the nature of god
or some such matter of concern
to those who don't have to live in poverty.

Literary middlemen find
native issues
are really much prettier

when defined and described
by non-natives.

Workers' rights are not of interest
to publishers and academics
so the question of censoring literature
completely concerned with union organizing
does not arise.

We, the censored,
are allowed voice
only to defend the oppressors.
We, the censored, cannot speak
against pornography.
Pornography is defended
by drunks and literary men,
and young women die
so that rich men can be free.

We, the censored,
are allowed to speak
in defence of the right of a rich Englishman
to write garbled books,
but we do not speak of the censorship
of half the population of Iran.

Half the population of Iran
cannot speak in public
or publish books
or even appear on the streets
looking like people.
Women made slaves
is not censorship;
it is merely a peculiar culture.

We, the censored,
cannot speak out for the women of Iran.

We do not know the details
of their slavery
because that information
is censored.

Freedom of speech is claimed
as a basic right of free men
even when they use this freedom
to silence their slaves.

Every ruling class practises censorship;
their lackeys defend this
by calling it freedom of speech
and surely everyone knows it's a joke
to talk about freedom of the press
when a few rich men own the media.
In the name of freedom of speech,
the hate-mongers own the streets
and we, the censored, are not even free
to tell them to shut up.

CENSORSHIP WORKS

History is written by the victorious ruling class
so history chronicles the lives of kings;
tells of greed, of brute behaviour
as if that was all that happened.
If that was all that happened,
we wouldn't be here.
Yet we are here in all our numbers
and in relative wealth.

We do not hear of the collective good;
we do not hear of the history of the world
which is cooperation in labour,
sharing of wealth
and communal care of children.

Dead soldiers are sometimes given voice.
Never have we heard from the serfs,
the peasants, the farmers of the world.
Witches are rarely given voice,
as are the mothers who raised sons for slaughter.
Never do we hear of the women
who did all the work.

We are trained to say that
hatred is truth
and love is lies
even though our own and every action
around us speaks the opposite.

Empires rise and fall;
love and labour go on forever.

Eavesdropping on Fourteen Bosses

Oh, for the life of a cladding man,
facing danger every day.
But a poor man goes where a poor man must
for the sake of higher pay.

While I was adding figures in Frank's office,
Don explained about the price of copper.
When it was high,
Granduc caused many men to build a huge building
near the BC-Yukon border.
When the price of copper dropped,
the camp was closed down.
The trouble was,
the building depended on being heated
to keep the snow sliding off
so without any heat
the weight of snow
collapsed the 800-million-dollar building.
While I was on the switchboard,
Don let me look at pictures
of metal ripped like cloth
by the massive snows of Stewart,
mangling steel like cloth.
The price of copper is up again;
the mine must now be repaired,
starting with cladders working for two months
on the mangled roof.
The repairs, like the shutdown, were to cost
some men's lives,
some men's health,
many people's hope
and fourteen million dollars.

Will he come home in a coffin,
or crippled by a fall?
Will he come home a drunkard?
Will he come home at all?

While I was taping blue strips
on a magnetic board in Norman's office,
Norman was calling the union office
to order seven men,
experienced in cladding,
delivered in two days to Stewart.
It's a hairy job, he said,
walking on steel girders 80 to 120 up
to clear away the crumpled pieces of roof.
If they're drinkers, they're in trouble, Frank said.
Last guy I sent up there beat up the bus driver
and was brought back in a strait jacket.
Lotta guys come back in strait jackets.
Not my problem, Norman said,
I wouldn't go up there myself.

Oh, for the life of a cladding man,
courting madness and a fall.
Will he come home in a wheelchair?
Will he come home at all?

There were guys fighting to go up there;
begging for a job, any job,
even 80 to 120 feet up on a mangled steel girder.
The only one who said
he would rather not go was Joe.
He had just got back from Princeton
and they gave him the rest of the day off
to go home and explain to his wife
he was leaving for Stewart in the morning.
While I was typing letters,
Joe asked me how he would explain to her.

Maybe she don't care, I said hopefully.
She cares, he said.

They pay them enough to drink with.
They pay them enough for drugs.
They pay them enough to tear them away
from the cloying of women's hugs.

They say women are masochists,
I said to Mary while filing,
but there is no woman I know of,
not one,
not now, not ever,
who would crawl around on steel girders
because of the price of copper.
Women don't get put in strait jackets;
they get tranquillized
or lobotomized
so they can wait quietly.

Will he come home in a coffin,
or injured in some brawl?
Will he come home a drunkard?
Will he come home at all?

Euthanasia Is Just Another Word for Murder

We want death to be pretty now
with a graceful exit
like some wrinkled ballerina
dancing off the stage.
We want death to be an event,
rather than a process.

So now along with the fear of dying
comes terror of the killers,
preparing evil potions.
Bland killers, bearing needles,
smiling,
as they stalk fading bodies,
to rob them of the process
of coming to terms with
that final fearful transition.

The other half want machines.
They want people who cannot die
although they will never live again.
Human bodies chained in pain
to machines,
like some bizarre rehearsal
for the torments of hell.
But taking away the machines
brings forth the murderous hordes
panting for the death of others,
yearning for the power of life and death
over certain powerless others.

Was it easy being born?
Was it quick and painless?
Is life easy?
Dignity is for funerals

and flowers.
Traumatized and screaming
we are brought forth
to live out the drama and adventure
of our years.
If we're lucky,
torment and discomfort
will help to separate us
from living;
pain and degeneration
will make death acceptable.
If we're lucky
we will die choking and gasping,
screaming of indignity,
whining of endings.
No one dies exactly right—
they die the wrong way,
in the wrong place,
and always
at the wrong time.

EVERY RICH MAN

Every rich man is sure
somebody else is getting more.
No matter how much he has,
someone else may be getting some
and he wants that too.
It's either women or Indians or Asians
or Blacks or Jews
or the Anthropophagi
who might be getting something,
the rich man wants.
If the poor are thrown a crumb,
the rich howl with rage.

There have been no real wars for years now.
In the last decade there have only been:
civil wars in Chad, Iran, Uganda,
El Salvador, Ethiopia and Haiti;
military coups in Turkey,
Liberia and Nigeria;
victories of sorts in Nicaragua, Iran and Uganda.
And there have been wars between Morocco and Zaire,
Iran and Iraq, Britain and Argentina,
Ethiopia and Sudan, China and Vietnam,
Kampuchea and Vietnam;
not to mention invasions
of Lebanon, Afghanistan and Grenada.
And there have been famines in Ethiopia,
Mali, Mauritania, Niger and Gambia;
massacres in Afghanistan, the Amazon regions,
Jonestown, Central African Republic, Uganda,
Botswana, Lebanon and East Timor.

The world has grown smaller.
In a time of great empires,
small nations must die.
Those who are not with us are against us.

In a conglomerate of clamouring needs,
it is hard to see that our fate, too,
is being settled in East Timor
and other wars considered minor.
We, too, are a small nation,
clinging feebly to a minor culture.
Our interest does not lie in
placating the giants

but in diplomatic folly
for the realization of the principle
of self-determination for all nations,
even East Timor,
even us.

November, 1988

Funny Way to Make a Living: CHOGM
(Commonwealth Heads of Government Meeting),
October, 1987

I was posted at the Hotel Vancouver
with the group making security passes for all the delegates
with the exception of the head of delegation and spouse.
The rest all stood in our lineup:
the ambassadors,
high commissioners,
cabinet ministers,
heads of armies.
Some minded; some did not.

We were untrained, unimpressive—
pushed through days of lectures
from assorted fools and liars
who told us nothing useful in three days of babbling.

Terrorists were mentioned only in passing
whereas we were warned repeatedly about the media.
Perhaps for government leaders
death is less fearful than exposure.

They don't care what you think about South Africa,
we were told,
the only question you'll be asked is:
where's the washroom?
In fact, they asked neither about the washroom
nor South Africa.

I chatted about plane flights and the weather
with various dignitaries;
saw the Duke of Edinburgh;
caught a glimpse of the Queen,
and various heads of government.

Once I found myself saying about a person
that he was nobody,
he was only a foreign minister.

The only really funny occurrence
was when the wife of a Canadian cabinet minister
introduced me to her husband.
She just knew he would be delighted to meet some temp
right after he had met twenty-seven prime ministers.
My best time was sharing fish and chips
with the protocol minister from Zimbabwe
at a takeout joint in the Royal Centre.
I tried not to appear too ignorant:
tried to memorize at least capitals and major religions;
learned how to pronounce Mashoeshoe,
King of Lesotho.
Where is Gambia?
Why were there delegates from Mozambique
when it was never a British colony?
How would you get to Vancouver
from the Solomon Islands?
Why was the laughter of the delegation from Zimbabwe
such a contrast to the solemnity of the others?

At first the vast rooms and high ceilings of the hotel
were intimidating, with sounds all bouncing around
or disappearing into carpets and damask curtains.
But then it got to be home:
all the pomp and glitter,
the array of uniforms,
the diamonds and tuxedoes.
I got to thinking I lived at the Hotel Vancouver
among the ornate columns,
silver settings,
crystal chandeliers.
And out on the street
was all the whistling and blowing

as heads of delegations came and went;
screaming of sirens,
rumble of motorcycles,
arrays of uniforms—
what a show.

Grand and glorious theatre it was.
I loved it.
But wondered at the same time:
don't grown men have anything better to do?

They were so pretty,
all decked out in the world's finest,
but don't they have anything better to do
than play games?

And ultimately, pomp and power
rest on cheap labour.
Besides us underpaid temps,
there were the cleaning and service staff of all the hotels;
all the service staff of the restaurants and shops;
and how many more hours of low pay
are needed to pay for just those uniforms?
All empires rest on the unpaid labour of peasants;
there is no other way to build an empire.

And on the streets, poor people paw through garbage.
I saw a beggar in a restaurant
fall upon food someone else had left half-eaten.
No motorcycle motorcade
for cheap labour,
just an assortment of beggars
to escort me home.

Don't ask what it cost
in human lives.

Don't ask who paid for those tuxedoes
in blood.
You can't stop it or start it
so enjoy the theatre.
The show is for you
and the show is all you're gonna get.

GENTLE LOVE OF MINE (AN ANTI-ROMANCE SONG)

Strong as a cowboy; every inch a real man
Summertime lover, you're gone again.

You loved me in summer when we laughed and were gay
but lost your desire on the first rainy day.
Poor macho cripple, I mistook for a man—
summertime lover; fair weather friend.

Sing me no sad songs of sentimental regret
for the girl left behind who you cannot forget.
Your songs never mention the children she raised
and for her abortions, there's no fine turn of phrase.

Sing me no sad songs of a good love gone wrong;
how we laughed and we loved all summer long.
Just go home to your first wife, my summertime man,
summertime lover; fair weather friend.

You know how to cheat; you know how to lie;
you know how to drink and you know how to die.
You can't raise your children; they don't know your name,
and you think that to love them is some dumb woman's
  game.

There's no room for me here, your needs never end;
when I need something, I ask a woman friend.
Unprepared for commitment, is your standard line
and then you go fishing, my summertime man.

Strong as a cowboy, my summertime man.

GOING TO THE DOCTOR

We must have gone by train;
how else was there to get to Grande Prairie?
But how did we get to the train?
I'm sure the school bus would have been too late.
Surely Art was too young
to drive the tractor on the main road?
Maybe we didn't go by train?
The only train ride I remember
was when we went to get the stitches removed
from where Art's finger used to be.
The trainman called Art "Stubby" and laughed.
Art thought the trainman was a jerk;
I stopped laughing right away.
Although Art was younger,
he was far more socially adept.
He was small and beautiful and clever;
I was overgrown and awkward
and stood around in corners sucking my thumb.
(Was that the thumb that was broken?)

When I got to see the doctor
and told him my thumb was broken,
he snorted, sneered and stamped his feet
simultaneously.
And what makes you think it's broken?
he asked, dripping disgust all over
the presumptuous, overgrown, child patient.
School nurse said it was, I replied.
(When I spoke at all in those days,
it had to be in short sentences.)
He sneered and snorted and stamped some more.
I saw right away that a mere nurse
should not have dared to diagnose.
Yet if the thumb wasn't broken,

I was in bad trouble.
Train money, lunch money, doctor money,
and no work done that day
for a thumb that turned out not to be broken?
And now, I also wonder, what school nurse?
We never had a school nurse.
Did some district nurse happen by
the day after my thumb got broken?
If so, it would have been a singular occasion
and ought to have been memorable.

So this doctor sent me for x-rays.
Now my mother had to pay the cost of x-rays
as well as the cost of the doctor,
the train money, the lunch money,
and a day with no work done.

Art and I walked over to the hospital
on a hot, dusty day
then we walked back to the doctor's office.
The thumb was broken.

I can't remember what treatment, if any,
was prescribed.
The doctor said we could hang around his office
until train time and I was grateful,
being hot and tired.
Art refused
so we had to wander the dusty streets some more.
Art said the doctor was a jerk
and he was right.
Upon retirement, the doctor went to be the head
of Moral Rearmament in the US,
having made a rather nice living
off injured children of subsistence farmers.

We must have looked into the jewellery store window
while wandering around.

They had a moving carriage and horses
in the window.
Whenever we were in Grande Prairie,
adults and children alike,
we would stop to marvel at this sight
of the tiny horses galloping
and the wheels turning on the tiny carriage.

How did we get home from the train?
I know: probably we had gone early
on our bikes and left them at the station.
It would have been exhausting
but wasn't that the norm for poor people
and their children?
Did the thumb hurt?
Was it splinted?
I shouldn't think one can milk cows
with a broken thumb?
I bet I ordered an open Denver sandwich for lunch.
I had an open Denver sandwich maybe three times,
and since I can't remember the occasions,
only the sandwiches,
this might have been one of them.

GREEN

We have walked through a green golden forest
seeking edible mushrooms in autumn;
chipping rock from the sides of green mountains;
picking berries on green summer days.

Once, camping at Casper Creek, we woke up to find
the truck surrounded by a minor lake—
drove to higher ground and in the morning looked down
at the green water churning at green banks.

Once, walking down a sun-striped, green-shaded trail,
swatting flies, listening to a busy little creek
somewhere far below, we saw a deer bounding
on rubber legs into the green bush.

The rain forest is a wall of lush green
with people-made paths peering out from between trees
and campsites tenuously crouched
at the edge of the solid green bush.

In the clearings, many-hued grasses flourish
and green-based wild flowers rampantly clash
colours with the surrounding trees—
waving stems of colour in the cool green breeze.

There are too many shades of green to be one colour;
there are ten greens in one leaf of skunk cabbage.
How many greens are in a cedar branch?
Many greens make a rain forest grow.

We have walked through the cool green forests
and slept under skies filled with stars;
we have walked on the sides of green mountains;
dipped our pails in the cool green streams.

HOUSEWORK

Although the kitchen floor
is only nine by six feet
and doesn't take long to wash,
I only wash it about once a week.
(While I was measuring the floor,
I saw that it was dirty.)
The bathroom is even smaller:
about 25 square feet.
I'm as good an average woman as any if
you ignore the fact I don't have children,
so if we go by me,
the average woman washes no more
than about 80 square feet a week.
At that rate it would take the average woman
about 10 years to wash an acre,
or even more formidable,
two billion years to wash BC.

But suppose I was not washing alone.
There are probably half a million
adult women in Vancouver
and although most of them have bigger floors,
and some may wash them more often,
if we each washed 80 square feet a week,
we could wash BC in 5,000 years.
The Pacific Ocean presents more of a challenge
but if those same people who are into washing floors
more than once a week, got together
only 40 billion of them could wash the Pacific
in a decade.
Women with children have to wash floors
way more often than the average woman
so it would take fewer of them
to do the same job.

What really needs doing is to wash North America;
but even those million women who read
Chatelaine in English every week
would take about 60,000 years
to wash North America.
Probably they should stick to doing only the parts
that really need cleaning, like New York,
Los Angeles, the Pentagon, Toronto,
and there's been a real stink
from Victoria lately.

Then there's laundry,
measurable for those of us
who still have clothes lines.
I wash only about a mile of clothes a year,
so it would take me some thousands of lifetimes
to hang all my laundry on the equator.
If I had help from about 25,000 others,
we could have clean underwear flapping
across the equator
in merely one year
and if all those million women
reading *Chatelaine* in English
did their washing,
we could have clothes hanging all along the Equator
in merely two weeks.
Then if you add the number of hours
an average Canadian watches TV
there'd be too many clothes to hang from the Equator;
the overflow would have to go
on the International Date Line
and there would probably still be some
left to put in the dryer.
And all that does not take diapers into consideration.
It would take only about 5,000 women with children
to clothespin across the Equator in a year.

Now on to cleaning bathrooms.
We have already washed the floor
so there's only the sink, tub and toilet left
if you ignore the walls
which I generally do
except when my sister is coming for Christmas.
Another consideration is windows.
The window space in our house
exceeds the floor space by a factor of 2.38;
however, the frequency of washing the floor
exceeds that of washing the windows
by a factor of 15.3956
so, in general, it can safely be said
that no matter how often windows are washed,
the sky will never be clean.

I have left out vacuuming completely.
The average woman (me) never does vacuuming any more.
The average woman writes silly poems
to prove God is a woman
because volcanoes are only a pot boiling over
on the Celestial Stove
and earthquakes are when She
decides to move the furniture
and clean behind it
for a change.

I Don't Write Anti-War Poems

I don't write anti-war poems
because I am not in principle
opposed to war:
it's just that I haven't seen a war
that made sense.

It seems to me, the wars of my lifetime
have all been the rich attacking the poor.
The rich take everything
and if the poor try
to keep something for themselves,
they get
a storm of death from the skies.

IF MY LOVE MADE ANY DIFFERENCE

If my love made any difference
you'd never know a day of pain.
If my love made any difference,
you would never cry again.

You would live to be a hundred
and never know a day of pain
and if my love made any difference,
you would never cry again.

Your days would all be filled with sunshine
unless, of course, you wanted rain,
but if my love made any difference,
you would never cry again.

IF YOU CAN'T BEAT THEM DOWN ANY OTHER WAY, TELL 'EM THEY'RE CYNICAL

When he says: I was just 17 years old and not ready to be a
  father,
that's sad.
When she points out she was also 17 years old and not
  ready to be a mother but was left to bring up the baby,
that's cynical.

When he says she and the kid on welfare get almost as
  much as he does working,
that's the truth, baby.
When she says: but there's two of us and one of you and it's
  your kid too,
that's cynicism.

When he says he loves her just to get her into bed,
  that's ordinary.
When she says: you're just saying you love me in order to
  get me into bed,
that's cynicism.

When he says he's not capable of involvement or prepared
  for commitment,
that's honesty.
When she says: you're an emotional cripple incapable of
  involvement or commitment,
that's cynicism.

When he says there is no revolution without the
  participation of women,
that's socialism.
When she says: yeah but maybe we'll have one without the
  participation of men,
that's cynicism.

When men can't tell the difference between sex and
 violence,
boys will be boys, you know.
And when women and children must be locked up to keep
 men from hurting them,
that's life.

When he says he's only interested in sex, not her,
that's honesty.
When she says she's only interested in sex, not him,
she's a ball-breaking, castrating, cold-hearted witch, and a
 nymphomaniac.

When he says the magic is over,
that's unfortunate for him.
When she says she loved him, not the magic,
that's tough for him too.

When he says he'll love her when she's old and grey,
 that's generosity.
When she says: given the statistics, when I'm old and grey,
 you'll be dead,
that's cynicism.

When he leaves her and doesn't tell her he's not coming
 back so she won't cry,
that's kind.
When she cries even worse because he didn't even say
 good-bye,
who cares.

If You Take the Pill
(to be sung to the tune of "The Old Grey Mare")

If you take the pill, you will likely suffer nausea,
If you take the pill, you might gain a lot of weight.
If you have asthma, your asthma might get worse.
But that's just a minor side-effect.

If you take the pill you might get jaundiced and
or require surgery for gall bladder disease.
Or you might just lose some hair and grow some cataracts
or some other of the minor side effects.

If you take the pill, you'll get more yeast infections
which will make you tired, itchy and irritable.
If you take the pill, your breasts might hurt a lot.
or you might just suffer from dizziness.
If you take the pill, your skin might turn blotchy brown;
it might be temporary or it might be permanent.
Your periods might stop or you might bleed all the time.
Or you might suffer from frequent urination.
If you take the pill, you might get all bloated up,
your ankles might swell up, your breasts might get
   enlarged.
You might develop high blood pressure from water
   retention.
It's all just a minor side effect.

If you take the pill, you'll probably get depressed;
you might feel a little down or you might feel very bad.
You might try, you might succeed, in committing suicide,
but that's just a minor side effect.

If you're a little weird, you might get a lot more weird;
you could start hearing things, you could start seeing
   things.

If you get migraine headaches, the pill will make them
  worse.
If you don't have headaches, the pill might bring them on.
If you have a headache, don't let it bother you;
it's only a minor side effect.

Taking the pill enhances growth of fibroids;
these are benign tumours which grow on the uterus.
The cure is menopause or hysterectomy,
but that's just a minor side effect.

Major side effects are strokes and heart disease;
major side effects are pulmonary emboli.
The chances increase with age and smoking
so you should quit smoking right away.
(And maybe lie about your age.)

Then your risk of death from blood clots will diminish
but you might grow a liver tumour which ruptures and
  hemorrhages
or you might get kidney disease or kidney failure
but then again, you might not.

I Went to Work

I went to work just a week ago,
the boss said: Honey, gonna let you go—
  We've got a lot of unemployment now;
  a lot of unemployment now.
We've got to change with the times as I'm sure you know,
with new machines and part-time workers, gotta let you go.
  I really hate to say it but you're unemployed right now.

I loved that job and I thought it would last.
My kids need shoes and my car needs gas,
  but there's a lot of unemployment now;
  a lot of unemployment now.
Four years sure count for something; two weeks' severance
  pay
and fifteen minutes to get my stuff and go away
  and a boss who says he's sorry that I'm unemployed right
  now.

I don't want jewels and castles in Spain;
I just want to eat and stay out of the rain.
  There's a lot of unemployment now;
  a lot of unemployment now.
There's something wrong with these times, I know that's
  true
and I won't work for nothing like they want me to do
  even though there's a lot of unemployment now.

with Maggie Benston

52

JOB INTERVIEW

Do I have any questions?
Yes, I do. Can I sing?

I won't often take a lunch break;
I know that's what's expected;
I know I'm not allowed to talk
or leave my working station.
I know there'll be no coffee breaks;
I know the pay is dismal.
But can I sing? Can I sing?
While I'm working, can I sing?

There's a law forbidding singing
in the Sultanate of Oman
but this is a democracy
and I have the right to vote.
Can I sing?

The price of my labour to you is cheap;
to me, it's dear.
But surely in hard times like these
I'm willing to be grateful
that I'm allowed to work for you
to age and sicken in your service,
if while I'm working I can sing.
Can I sing? Can I sing?

In the windowless and airless rooms
that office workers work in,
I'll sing of space and air and sand
and snow falling on the ocean.
I'll dream of love and picket lines
and sing. I'll remember one night
we camped by Anderson Lake

when the moon was full.
I'll conjure up hot-blooded
sexual fantasies and/or memories.
I'll sing of jacaranda trees
of Cairns in northern Queensland.
I'll hum while remembering
the gleaming gold cupolas
of the Kievpecharsk Monastery
overlooking the Dnieper River.
I'll chant quietly of all the babies I ever held;
the children I spent time with.
I might remember in slow motion detail
walking to the park with Angela one summer day.
I might sing of cherry blossoms
drifting down like pink snow.

Other times, I might sing about
rain pounding on the windows
while my beloved snores beside me.
I'll remember walking through pine forests
in search of matsutake and chanterelles
with leaves and needles crunching underfoot
and autumn wind ruffling my hair.
I'll ponder the awful faith of planting seeds
and expecting them to grow up vegetables.

I'll dream of full moon on Anderson Lake
and sing. I'll dream of love
and picket lines, and sing.
Can I sing? Can I sing?

LAYOFFS

When layoffs are a rumour
half the people are terrified
they'll lose their job;
the other half are terrified
they won't.

They all go in the end:
the ones eager to go,
the back-stabbers,
the good workers and the bad workers,
all poisoned by living with fear.

Even when you're laid off together
you leave one by one
to whatever individual fate you can seek and find
out there.

Everyone feels they have failed;
feels they could have controlled their destiny;
feels the fate beyond their reach
could have been grasped
if they tried hard enough.

The days of hope and terror now ended
in a flood of tears,
some go berserk; some go catatonic,
living with the screaming fear of no pay cheque.
For the survivors,
there's a certain breadth of vision:
horizons beckon through the mist
of tears.

LOST IN THE WOODS

There was a swamp where
I thought the road would be.
Working my way around the swamp,
I walked through endless bush,
eventually coming upon a canyon
where somewhere far below
there was a waterfall.

There is nothing in the forest
that is anything like me.
Nothing that even knows I'm there
or knows, let alone cares,
if I live or die.
All the things we consider essential
like time and place and pain and joy
are meaningless there.
Fortunately, I panicked
and filled with my ragged sobbing breath
the fearful, inhuman silence.

I was trained by the best
in the theories of foundness
so with only sometimes faltering faith
I was able to work my way out
to the road.

But now being lost
crouches behind my brain
disturbing my work
until sometimes I think that
if I didn't love my husband
and if I didn't have a computer
I would go again to the bush
to find that terrible silence.

But most of the time
I think with bitterness and shame that,
although I am a person who loves clichés
and wants most of all to be ordinary
and although I was lost
for three days panic time
(only half an hour earth time),
not once
did I walk in circles.

MAGGIE

Good-bye old friend
Long time friend
Now beyond time

Never pick up the guitar
Sing like an angel
Sing on the picket lines
Sing to soothe a friend
Now beyond comfort

Never for walks
Good road you travelled
Now beyond distance
Long road without you

No more talk
No more papers
Ideas are for living
Students to other classes now

Never for dinner
Life no longer needs sustaining
The earth now your home
Return to the earth
Return to the air
Return to the wind and the sea

Good-bye friend
Never helped you live
Couldn't help you die
Now beyond pain

Never bring you daffodils
Now beyond season

March, 1991

MALANKA

"May the rye and wheat multiply and ripen
and the pasture grasses grow...",
goes the old New Year's greeting.

Then the left-wing Russian/Ukrainian choir
sang: "Rejoice Oh Earth
for Christ is born."
To think that in my 48th year,
this would come to pass.
I used to sing in that choir decades ago
when they were politically correct;
and now they sing about Christ,
for chrissake.

I asked an old man to explain.
He said he's 82 this year
although in English, he's only 81.
He said he's got some Siberian tea
for longevity.

But what about that choir?
I used to sing in that choir.
Finally he relents:
The old gods have died, he says,
now they seek older gods.

January, 1988

MODERN OFFICE

You know, I'd rather see the sunshine;
I would rather hear the rain.

What right have I to imagine
there are seasons there outside?
There are no seasons, only fiscal years;
there is no sun although spring is here.
There are no dreams, only doubts and fears,
and the phone that buzzes all day.
Just the phone that buzzes all day, all day,
just the lights that shine bright and hot all day,
and the lovers who came and went away,
and the phone that buzzes all day, all day,
yes, the phone that buzzes all day.

You know, I'd rather see the sunshine;
I would rather hear the rain.

There are no days and there are no nights;
just the airless rooms and the blinding lights
and the phone that buzzes all day, all day,
and the friends who died or moved away
and the high demands for the meagre pay
and the phone that buzzes all day, all day.
The desks are crowded into airless rooms;
the windows are sealed and tinted in gloom.
There is no sun and there is no rain
just fear of unemployment, poverty and pain,
and the phone that buzzes and buzzes all day,
yes, the phone that buzzes all day.

There are a lot of different dungeons;
there are many kinds of pain.

ODE TO OVERPOPULATION

Babies—
we need more babies,
more and more and more
babies.

Yes, but—
all those mouths to feed.
All those mouths to feed?
No—
all those hands to work.

There are too many capitalists
and too few babies.
There is too much money spent on telling farmers
not to grow wheat
and not enough on babies.
There is too much time spent worrying about how to stop
the poor from breeding,
and not enough time spent making babies.

We should have more babies.
Lots of babies:
brown babies,
black babies
yellow babies
red babies
fat babies
thin babies
short babies
long babies
hairy babies
bald babies
cute babies

icky babies
toothless babies
babies with blue eyes
babies with brown eyes
happy babies
cranky, colicky babies
sweet babies
sad babies
silly babies—

What the world needs is
fewer capitalists
and more babies.

ON AGING

Whose skin is this?
It's far too big for me
and has to sag down
in folds that get pinched.
Someone else must have
my well-fitted skin.

Whose breasts are these?
Mine moved with the rest of my body;
they never flopped around
like poached eggs on a plate,
nor caught in my armpits
when I'm turning over in bed.

Some old turkey must have got my neck
'cause I sure got his.

Surely these are not my joints—
aching and creaking and burning like fire.
My joints, like my breasts,
were part of my body
and did their job without calling attention.

Whose friends are these—
wrinkling and greying
and falling prey to major diseases.
My friends were supple and energetic,
and given to talking of illness
as a fascinating theory.

Whose husband is this?
Limping and complaining
and with his hairline receding
faster than he can walk.
Who's got my handsome green-eyed lover?

Good old feet,
at least I recognize them.
Bony and painful
with long crooked toes—
those are my feet all right.

ON BEING FIRED

I can't remember their names any more;
I can't remember their names any more;
they came and they went, never asking what for,
and got eaten by the people-eating machine,
while money runs like blood to secret coffers.

In the belly of the beast,
you can hear young women laughing,
laughing, laughing....
In the belly of the beast,
you will never hear them cry.

I like me, I'm strong; I can live here all right.
I've worked here two years, a week, and a day.
It keeps me off welfare and food lineups,
while money runs like blood to secret coffers.

They came from Toronto, the young hatchet women.
And I thought I was getting hard.
Geez, you know, I thought I was getting hard!
I am but a novice
fit only to crouch at their stone feet,
yearning after their stone heart.

In the belly of the beast,
you can hear young women laughing,
laughing, laughing....
In the belly of the beast,
you will never hear them cry.
No, you'll never hear them cry.
Nor me either.
You won't hear me crying.

On Skateboarding

Amazing how good those boys are at it:
leaping and dancing and swirling.
Must have taken a long time to get that good.
I suppose they spend
all their leisure hours
skateboarding.

But where are the girls?
I suppose the girls
are cooking and cleaning.
I suppose they're talking about love,
giggling about which boy is the cutest,
how to make relationships work.
It's all necessary training for adulthood
whereas skateboarding is preparation
only for skateboarding.
Even girls talking fashion and makeup
is more useful than boys skateboarding.
The girls prepare for marriage and parenting;
the boys prepare for
skateboarding.

And
oh my god
those girls
will have to marry
those boys.

PEACE, THEY SAY

Peace, they say, and I think of
five million dead Ukrainians.

Peace, they say, and I think of India
where English domination
brought an end to war,
a beginning to famine.

Peace, they say, and I think of
the Canadian prairies
where no more wars were fought
after the conquerors came.
The natives died of famine and smallpox,
and in peace, their population dropped
to one tenth.

The Aztecs were bloody emperors:
blood-covered priests cut living hearts
from prisoners of war.
The people rose to help the Spanish
against the Aztec tyrants.
The Spanish conquest brought peace
and all the people died.
There are no survivors to tell
how the people died.

It is slow to kill people one at a time.
Massacres only increase the birth rate
and even bombs are slow.
The only way to wipe out
nations and classes and races
is to take away
people's means of livelihood.

No horrors to terrify the children of the rulers,
no guilt to expiate,
no trials to be held at Nuremberg.

They don't call it war
when workers die of working.
Only when workers are heard protesting
is the peace shattered.

They don't call it war
when women do all the work
for none of the money.
It isn't war when veiled women
are locked into their working prisons.
When the witches were burned,
it was peacetime.
There is no war in Guyana now.
The Beothuks suffer war no more.
Is there a war in Mali?
I think not, for every second baby dies.

Peace, land, and bread
is what the Russian peasants asked for
and received through war.
Now they need another war for wages,
for victory,
for meat and vegetables to go with the bread.

April, 1988

68

REBEL

You should curl your hair, she said.
My hair is curly, I replied.
She said it would look nicer if I curled it every night in
  rollers.
She said it was a shame nice hair was wasted on me.

She didn't mention my bitten fingernails—
her nail polish was chipped;
her nails were not perfectly symmetrical.
Uneven, unpolished nails are ugly—
ugly, ugly, ugly.
Nothing good will ever happen to you
if your fingernails aren't right.

You should hem your skirt better, she said.
You should make the hemming invisible.
That takes time, I said, and, besides, I don't know how.
She said she could show me.
I said I already know how to type
and I can do books
and I have a class four driver's license;
I knit and I crochet,
and I know about spelling and grammar
have a familiarity with medical, legal and insurance terms;
I have a degree in Sociology (first class honours)
and I was a lab technician
and I've had some books published
and I can handle a switchboard
and I still play softball even though my dentist said I was too
  old.
She said I better learn to hem my skirt.

Nothing good will happen to you
if you don't learn to hem your skirt.

You won't get a job
and you can't get married
and you can't have babies
and they'll cut you off unemployment insurance
and your daddy won't let you come home
and they'll send you to a shrink
who will lock you up.
They will let you on welfare
if you admit you are sick
instead of insisting all that is really wrong
is you wouldn't learn to hem your skirt.

I wonder why I do it, she sighed,
tweezing her eyebrows.
I wonder if it's worth it—
my life spent before mirrors.
You are beautiful, I said,
you would be beautiful anyway.
She sighed, disbelieving,
and went back to tweezing,
teasing,
plucking,
squeezing,
powdering,
combing,
polishing,
trimming.

There may be people starving;
there may be revolutions brewing;
there are famines and epidemics
and the danger of nuclear holocaust.
That's not for us to worry about.
Our life depends on how we look.
Our fate depends on hemming a skirt
and curling our hair.
They are killing people in Brazil.

Women in Iran and Saudi Arabia are being tortured.
There is a war in Yugoslavia.
You need to worry about your hair.
Get it styled,
get it permed,
get it dyed,
get it curled,
get it straightened,
get it streaked.

If they can make you tear out your eyebrows
they can also make you work for nothing.
They can even make you exploit those other people.
They can make you do anything
while chasing false dreams.
Think you'll meet some rich husband?
Do you really want a man
who wants a woman
dressed like that?
You think it's your fingernails
keeping you from promotion?
You won't get promoted anyway—
you're a woman.

There ought to be some advantage
to lack of power
like wearing whatever we like.
Let's quit worrying about hems
and progress to worrying about child care.
Let's get out there
and alter their perceptions
instead of ourselves.
And if they can't be altered,
let's ignore them
and slouch around in
shoes that are shaped like feet,
clothes that feel good.

Men might beat us;
women might revile us,
but who knows?
They might, instead,
join us.

RETROSPECTIVE

The Ukrainian Canadian experience
was being abandoned in the immense bush
with no tools, no roads, no schools, no hospitals,
nothing.

The Ukrainian Canadians were homesteaders
and some found prosperity
and some found early graves.
The Ukrainian Canadians were itinerant labourers
and some found prosperity
and some found early graves.
The Ukrainian Canadians were domestic labourers
and none found prosperity
and some found better jobs
and some found early graves.
All found bitterness
as immense as the uncleared bush.

Those who died old in bed later
cohabited uneasily with mega-farms,
rarely visited by grandchildren
with unpronounceable names
clacking away in a foreign tongue.
You have to talk to them as carefully
as if they were English,
these non-Ukrainian descendents
of my foremothers.

Sometimes now someone tells me
their grandfather was Ukrainian.
They look puzzled and resentful
as they say this.

Then their eyes light up.
Perogies, they say confidently.
Sometimes I tell them the letter "g"
is almost never used in Ukrainian
but usually I don't.
Urban cowboys,
perogy Ukrainians.

SCIENTISTS INVENT RACE

Until about three hundred years ago,
race was of no interest.
All foreign lands were thought to be populated
by ogres and monsters and Anthropophagi
so merely a different skin colour
was not remarkable.
Even the Greeks and the Romans
who were excessively disturbed
by "otherness"
did not link it to biology.
Slaves were still the same colour
as their masters.

It was white slave owners
of black slaves
who needed to buy science and religion.
The Pope approved the subjugation of non-Christians;
scientists developed the theory
that human beings
are naturally and permanently
comprised of separate races;
that race can be measured and verified
and described and named.

Of course, race is easier
said than done.
The material is obstreperous.
Some people just won't fit into the race
to which they are seen to belong.
Differences between individuals
of the same race
are greater than the differences
between races.
But if race cannot be discovered,
it must be invented.

It's a faith.
If race did not exist,
how then would the choice be made
of who will be forced to labour
their entire generations
for the benefit of others?

The estimates of the number of races
have ranged from two—
the Handsome and the Ugly—
to over sixty.
Science has now decreed
there are either eight or nine,
although there might be five or four,
or some other number entirely.

To scientifically quantify race,
anthropometry used to be big—
measuring heights and proportions and heads—
until it was discovered
these differences were nutritional, not hereditary.
Metabolism and rates of growth
differ among different people
but these also change
with a change of environment.

All human blood is the same
in all components.
No matter how many studies are done,
no differences have been discovered.
The incidence of blood groups varies somewhat
but this is independent of skin colour.
You can't tell a person's race
from a skeleton.

Individual brain sizes vary so much
you can't tell what race
any given brain comes from.

Brain size, in any case,
has no relationship
to intellectual ability.

Hair colour is supposed to go along
with skin colour
but it doesn't always.
Red hair cannot be explained.

Eye colours are named arbitrarily
because they are too difficult to record.
Different studies use different arbitraries
and are, therefore, not useful.

When occasionally scientists consider noses
they say the long European nose
is to warm up cold air
before it reaches the lungs.
The flat faces and small noses
of northern Chinese and Japanese
are because of the cold.
So there.

Culture comes from a people's history,
not from their colour.

This leaves only a single characteristic
by which to determine race
and that is skin colour.
Skin colours of human beings
go from light to dark
with all the shades in between;
there isn't a place you can stop and say:
now this is a new skin colour.

But how can you have racism
without race?
Having lost the obvious,

the scientists turn
in desperation to earwax.
Earwax is judged to be
either dry-flaky or sticky-moist.
Urine is also analyzed
for excretion of certain amino acids.
This is progressive and scientific:
the science of race has progressed beyond
crude observation of appearance
to crude observation of earwax.

If races were pure and separate
and developed in isolation from each other,
then it would follow
that language would also so develop
and that scientists would be
happily studying languages
to find out where
people came from and when
and where they went after that
and where they stayed forever.
Alas, this is not to be.
Languages are even more obstreperous
than the human material.
The Bushmen, for example,
have twelve or more languages,
each unintelligible to the other.
If Bushmen are not a single unified group
which developed in splendid isolation
where does that leave the race theory?

The overlapping and intermixing of peoples
is never considered significant.
Scientists are too busy
trying to separate
to notice the mingling.

It seems obvious
to even the most educated observer
that the history of humanity
is the story of movement.
Some of our ancestors stayed home,
but most went back and forth
and around and about
and that's history.

Some scientists try to show
that certain races stand higher
on the scale of evolution
than others.
Other scientists scorn
such obvious racism.
But why would you separate people
if not to proclaim
one group better than another?

All people are the same and
all people are different.
For purposes of racism, however,
the likenesses have to be ignored
and the differences made into criteria
for grossly differing wage rates.
If race does not exist,
we will invent it.

All the arguments to prove the inferiority
of certain "races" have also been used
to prove the inferiority of women.
Women have always been
forced to do more of the work
for less of the resultant goods and services.
Artificial boundaries among people
are to extend "natural" poverty
to a defined group

so that a self-defined and self-selected group
can perpetuate its "natural" wealth.

Workers now have to be paid—
the question, for imperialism,
is not How much?
but, How little?

If race did not exist,
cheap labour would have to be redefined
every generation.
Bigger armies and more police
cost immense amounts of money;
a few fraudulent scientists
look like a bargain by contrast.

The race theory also helps
to send soldiers off to kill
for god and country,
but mostly, for wealth.
You can't kill people;
they first have to be redefined
as something other than us.

Sometimes they show us dying babies
on television and we don't go crazy.
It's them, not us;
their babies, not ours.

The poor and disinherited
are supposed to see their destiny
in their skin colour and not ask about
the colour of money,
the colour of guns,
the colour of imperialism.
It is not for our benefit,
the quantifying and obfuscating.

Blood and bones
and sweat and pain
don't have a race.

Blood and bones and sweat
are the same.
Only the wealth is different.
It's not so much a matter of skin colour
as the colour of famine,
the colour of stolen land,
the colour of cheap goods and services.

SUPERVISOR: any person given small power
ANDREA
EVELYN
FROUIDA
ANNETTE
Twenty-one other women of varying ages and colours
One man in a suit and about three men in coveralls

TIME: 1982
SETTING: Office with twenty-five typewriters lined up—two rows of ten down the middle at an angle and three on each side, one of which is larger than the others. There is a low screen between the two rows of desks and a large clock on the wall.

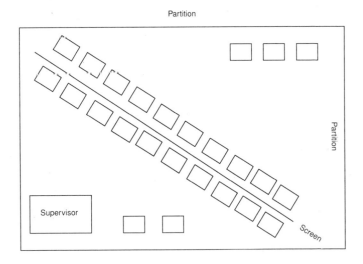

I

ANDREA and EVELYN walk to opposite front edges of the stage.

ANDREA: That summer of the layoffs,
  I was trying to organize us into a union...

EVELYN: And I was chasing men...

ANDREA: Without much success...

EVELYN: Without much success, until....

ANDREA: We work, that's what we do;
  We dream, that's what we do.
  In good times, we dream of better jobs,
  more pay, a nice boyfriend.
  In bad times, of any job,
  even this one.

EVELYN: Some of us just want the nice boyfriend.

*The clock shows 8:45. Women are drifting in, some chattering
together, some coming in singly. They put their purses and other
bags in their desk drawers, talking while doing so, and then
gather at the three small desks arranged at one end of the room.
They are saying things like:*

  ...family dinner...
  Bobby had a sore throat...
  ...got all my baking done...
  ...sewing a new outfit for my niece...

*ANDREA and EVELYN walk over and join the group. ANDREA
hands out union leaflets but no one reads them. They drift
around talking and put the leaflets in purses, drawers or
pockets. ANDREA starts talking to EVELYN. Soon the background*

voices diminish as EVELYN and ANDREA's conversation attracts their interest.

ANDREA: Well, I thought about putting an ad in the paper, but have you seen the ads lately. Ugh!

EVELYN: Dolly is bugging me to go to an agency. They're supposed to match you with one guy a week. Dolly just wants to do it to get lots of dates. You know how she is...

FROUIDA: Why don't you just go to those singles places?

ANDREA and EVELYN laugh.

FROUIDA: Aren't there those nightclub kind of places and pubs and that sort of thing? Sometimes when we go with my husband, there seems to be a lot of men by themselves.

ANDREA and EVELYN laugh again.

ANDREA: Have you ever met any of them?

EVELYN: First of all, they're married. You can't tell the married ones from the single ones. And they're after one thing. Right now. Before they even tell you their name, or instead of telling you their name....

ANDREA: I always ask them for their phone number when they ask for mine. They get really upset.

ANNETTE: *(shocked)* Whatever would you do that for?

ANDREA: That way you get some clue if they're married, if they won't give you their home phone number. Although one did and I called and a woman answered the call and says I'll give my husband the message.

84

EVELYN: They talk about chains and things. They say they're not ready for commitment. They're just ready for one thing.

ANDREA: And if you ask them who do they think they are anyway, they start calling you names. Or they cry. Or they cry and call you names. Have you ever met one who didn't cry, Evelyn?

EVELYN: Then there's AIDS. There's still herpes. They're all drunk.

ANDREA: So what? So are you.

EVELYN: Shut up! Witch!

FROUIDA: I thought AIDS was only for those men, you know....

EVELYN: I don't know, they say not. They used to say that if you slept with a person you slept with everybody he slept with in the last year. Now they're saying five years. I heard seven years the other day.

FROUIDA: *(patting EVELYN comfortingly)* Well, it's not something to worry about.

EVELYN: All very well for you to talk! You're not on the front lines!

ANDREA: Speaking of front lines, we should join the union before...

ANNETTE: It's already too late. I heard it's starting this morning.

The clock shows 8:59. The women all sit at their desks and turn on their typewriters. Each typewriter has a pile of forms sitting beside it all lined up exactly and all exactly the same height. Each of the typists puts a form in her typewriter and exactly at 9:00, they all start typing.

The SUPERVISOR comes in, goes to her desk and surveys the room from there. The typists are all typing away, heads down, backs straight. SUPERVISOR walks up to five women one after the other, leans over and says something quietly to them. Each stops typing, and stands up, and then they all follow the SUPERVISOR out. The remaining typists do not look up or pause in their typing.

The SUPERVISOR comes back and takes the piles that were beside the typewriters of the five women who have left and distributes them among the remaining typists.

Some men in coveralls come in and dismantle five of the desks and carry them out. The typing does not pause.

II

8:15. There are now only twenty typewriter stations, and the partition on the right has been moved to make a smaller space.

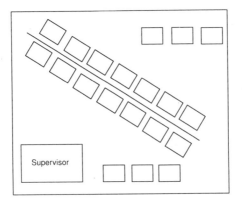

FROUIDA walks to the centre of the stage.

FROUIDA: And so it began, the summer of the layoffs.
　　　　　Each of us hoped we wouldn't be next.
　　　　　Even when my best friend was laid off,
　　　　　all I thought is I hope I won't be next.
　　　　　The trouble is, the piles of forms
　　　　　block the view. And even dreams
　　　　　shrink to fit onto preprinted forms.
　　　　　I dream that my crippled child will walk;
　　　　　I dream my other child will excel
　　　　　in school or in sports.
　　　　　I dream my husband will make a lot of money.
　　　　　And all the time, I type the forms
　　　　　and think that with no job security,
　　　　　the dreams are faded and dirty
　　　　　like a form with too many corrections,
　　　　　and you have to tear it up,
　　　　　enter the number in the book
　　　　　and start again clean,
　　　　　if you can.

The women come in as before, talking to each other, but they are not animated now, they move slower, and, of course, there are fewer of them. FROUIDA joins them.

　　　　　She cried and cried....
　　　　　Alice has a new job already....
　　　　　...severance pay, unemployment insurance....
　　　　　Gudrun wishes she had left earlier....

ANDREA and EVELYN stroll in, looking happy and relaxed in contrast to the tension and depression of the others.

ANNETTE: All very well for them—no family to support.

FROUIDA: But they're trying...they're trying.

Everybody laughs.

FROUIDA: You found the one yet?

ANDREA says no but EVELYN looks smug.

EVELYN: *(to ANDREA)* Don't tell them.

ANDREA: Oh no! I wouldn't dream of telling! After all, it's disgusting to have gone to a dating agency. It indicates a certain level of desperation you're never supposed to admit. I know! Tell them you met him while he was dead drunk on the pub floor. That's respectable. *(Turns to the other women)* So there's this guy, dead drunk on the barroom floor, Evelyn picks him up, hoses him down, drives him home and now she has a date for every night this week.

FROUIDA: What's he like? Is he nice?

EVELYN: As nice as any drunk on the pub floor can be. *(Laughs)* Actually, he's very nice.

FROUIDA: Not married.

EVELYN: Well, he is actually. His wife doesn't live with him though. She was really the drunk, not him.

ANDREA: He left her because she was a drunk?

EVELYN: No, actually, she left him. She ran away with the next-door neighbour. I gather he was a drunk too.

FROUIDA: Any children?

EVELYN: No, not John. The next-door neighbour had children though.

ANDREA: I hate to interrupt this romance here, but we should talk about layoffs and union.

She hands everyone a leaflet. The women take them but don't read them, just stand around awkwardly holding the leaflets. The SUPERVISOR comes in, and the leaflets disappear into handbags or under piles of paper. They sit at their desks and promptly at 9:00 a.m., the typewriters all start up.

A man in a suit comes in and calls away seven of the women. The typewriters falter now and then as the remaining women watch the typewriters being moved out and the desks dismantled. The SUPERVISOR patrols the aisles. Whenever someone turns her head to watch the desks being moved, the SUPERVISOR walks over and raps her fingers on that typist's desk. Every minute or so she shouts: "GIRLS! TALKING!"

III

8:45. Partition has been moved to shrink the typing space some more. There are only thirteen typewriters left now.

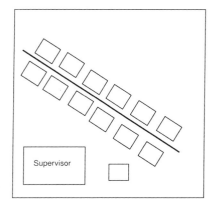

ANNETTE goes to the front of the stage.

ANNETTE: I would have liked to join them,
       young, white and energetic,
       talking union, talking men.

But each day starts too early
and ends too late.
My only goal is to stay awake.
So that's all I do all day,
think about raising children
on a typist's pay
and concentrate
on not falling asleep.

The women come in studying leaflets. Sighs and paper rustling.

...we should have done it earlier...
...other departments won't join though....
...too scared.....

ANDREA: We could still join. There are still thirteen of us left.

ANNETTE: By tomorrow there won't be.

FROUIDA: Union means strike.

ANDREA: Strike is better than layoff. Strike means a job, more money, more job security.

FROUIDA: Union means strike.

ANDREA: There were no strikes in Uganda, were there? No strikes, no hospitals, poor roads, no schools...and everything that goes with no union and no strike. No old age pension, not even a telephone system. That's what goes with no strike.

ANNETTE: Gudrun got another job. If we join, we'll never get another job.

ANDREA: Susan and Eileen and Sarah haven't got another job yet.

90

ANNETTE: They get unemployment insurance.

ANDREA: How long will that last?

FROUIDA: Union means strike.

> ANDREA *throws up her hands in rage and stamps her feet.*
> EVELYN *comes in, looking so smug they all have to smile.*

ANNETTE: What love does for you!

FROUIDA: Getting married yet?

> EVELYN *just smiles smugly and puts down her purse on her desk.*

ANNETTE: Is your mother pleased?

> EVELYN *suddenly loses her smugness and collapses into a chair.*

EVELYN: She hates me. She hates John's mother.

ANDREA: Does John mind?

EVELYN: Oh, she *loves* John. None of it is John's fault. It's me who's going out with a married man. She goes on and on.

ANDREA: Why does she hate John's mother?

EVELYN: John's mother lives in John's house. Or maybe John lives in her house. Or maybe they share it. I don't know. John's mother has two dogs and a boyfriend named Tiger.

FROUIDA: She's not married?

EVELYN: No, and in fact she's trying to get rid of Tiger. But she can't because she co-signed a loan for him. So it must be her house, I just realized, otherwise, how could she co-sign a loan? So if she throws Tiger out and he doesn't pay the loan, she's out about $15,000.

ANNETTE: This Tiger sounds delightful.

EVELYN: So she has to buy him food and clothing and liquor—and how that man puts away liquor!—just to safeguard her investment.

FROUIDA: Hm. $15,000 to throw him out. How much to keep him?

EVELYN: She'd lose the house, you see. I know she doesn't have that kind of money.

ANDREA: What about John?

> *They look at the clock and sit down at their desks and start typing. After a while, a man in a suit comes in and calls seven of them away. The remaining women keep typing. Men come in and start dismantling and rearranging desks.*

IV

8:45. The desks have been rearranged to fit the smaller space. There are only six small desks left now. The other side of the partition is being used for storage and is full of boxes.

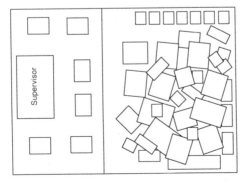

ANDREA walks to the front of the stage.

ANDREA: And I saw that the job was over
      and I thought maybe
      the next one would be better,
      if there was a next one at all.
      And I thought of all the years
      and all the jobs
      and of the years and jobs
      yet to come.
      If we don't make a stand,
      they will all slip away like this.
      We will always be going away like this,
      one by one,
      with only tears
      to light the way.

The women walk in silently and silently deposit purses and coats as appropriate. EVELYN comes in. They all turn to look at her hopefully but she is just as depressed as they are.

EVELYN: He's gone quiet. He watches and waits.

No one says anything. They stare at the floor or out the window.

EVELYN: He'll find something wrong with me, won't he? He's sure to find something. He'll say it's this or that, won't he? I'll believe him, won't I? There's always something.

ANNETTE: Are you being nice to him?

EVELYN: Does it matter what I do? He'll find something, won't he?

EVELYN sits down and stares at her typewriter. Looks around, seems confused that there are so few desks.

EVELYN: Where did everybody go?

ANDREA: We've got to plan our lives. Are we just going to let it happen? Are we going to drift along, let our jobs disappear and not lift one little finger?

FROUIDA: Union means strike.

ANDREA: Non-union means layoff.

EVELYN: John says they lay off at union places too.

ANDREA: There it's an orderly layoff with orderly recall.

EVELYN: That would be nice. To know... *(She trails off and stares into space.)*

ANDREA: Why won't you consider it then?

ANNETTE: You have to sign up everyone, not just the typists.

ANDREA: *(grimly)* I'm working on it.

ANNETTE: You can't do it though.

ANDREA: I could if you helped.

EVELYN: You don't understand. I don't give a shit about this job. This one or any other one. They're all the same. Those people who got laid off get a rest, while we get more and more work piled on us. No more coffee breaks now. Now the supervisor says we can't leave at 5 if there's still some typing left.

ANDREA: Those issues can be covered in a union contract.

EVELYN: I don't care about this job!

ANDREA: *(stung)* What about of those of us who do care?
And what about John? I suppose you don't care about him
either.

EVELYN: Don't be a creep!

Nine o'clock and they all start typing.

V

*Another 8:45 but the office is still empty. The six typists come in
about 8:56. They exchange brief good mornings but do not talk,
going straight to their typewriters and to work.*

*EVELYN comes in last, defeated and depressed, and goes to her
typewriter.*

ANDREA: Gone, eh?

*EVELYN nods, chokes. ANDREA reaches to pat EVELYN but just
then the SUPERVISOR strides in and seeing ANDREA reaching
towards EVELYN, veers to stride menacingly towards them.
ANDREA's hand drops from patting EVELYN, back to her
typewriter. EVELYN has apparently not even noticed ANDREA's
small attempt at a comforting gesture.*

*At 9:05 a man in a suit comes in and ANDREA is called out.
The others don't even look up. Other men come in and remove
ANDREA's desk. The others keep typing without a pause.*

EVELYN turns toward the front of the stage and walks forward.

EVELYN: So it was gone,
        my time for summer dreams.
        I hadn't been laid off then yet.
        Hundreds, no, more likely thousands by then
        but not yet me.

I was special.
Aren't we all special?
I fell in love.
Don't we all fall in love?

What I wanted was so ordinary.
How did ordinary desire for love and home
become an impossible dream
that summer of the layoffs?

Eventually, of course,
they came for my desk, too.
I guess I'll be reading the papers now—
want ads, the ones for jobs,
the ones for men,
the ones for cheap rooms.

I guess I'll get by somehow.
Don't we all get by somehow?
Dreaming of the past and future,
never of the present.

Never once did we,
do we,
look at each other,
talk about important things,
that summer of the layoffs.

SUMMER ROMANCE (ANOTHER ANTI-ROMANCE SONG)

It's winter now; the winter winds are cold,
the heater in the car is broken.
The winter skies pour sodden winter rain:
cold, soggy winter rain.
It's winter.

It's better than the waiting by the phone
those hot, hot summer days
when I loved you.

The wind blows cold, the bitter, winter wind,
my chronic smoker's cough is more chronic.
I have a cold and cold sores on my lips,
there's ringworm on my wrist
and my knees ache.

It's better than the sleepless summer nights,
the sleepy summer days
when I loved you.

The sky is grey, there's greyness in my soul,
I'm drinking in excess of moderation.
My teeth are stained and cavities abound;
I can't afford to see
a dentist.

It's better than those dreamy August days,
those steamy summer days
when I loved you.

I seem to have arthritis in my knees,
I'm broke and sick and poor this winter.
I drink and smoke what little bread I have
to ease the sullen ache
of winter.

It's better than the waiting by the phone
those hot, hot summer days
when I loved you.

THE ADVENTURES OF LEPINSKY IN POLAND (PRE-SOLIDARITY)

(based on a story told to me by Jim Chapman in March, 1989)

Why Lepinsky left his hometown, why his wife was English
  and how it came to be
that his brother was head of the secret police in Warsaw,
  is unknown to me.
The place Lepinsky was born was Poland
  then reverted to Ukraine
then Stalin decreed that the area was 80% Poles
  so it was made part of Poland again.
It's no good asking now
  if they were really Polish;
if Stalin said something,
  to question it was foolish.

Now Lepinsky owned about two hundred acres of bush
  in Castlegar and not much else
when he got a bright idea about making enough money
  to visit his relatives and birthplace.
The idea was to hire a surveyor to divide up his bush
  into four-acre plots
then to advertise in California or wherever
  of crazy city people there are lots.
Each time Lepinsky made a sale
  of another four-acre plot,
he could go home to Poland
  and play the big shot.

Lepinskys made another sale not that long ago
  so they made travel plans.
The wife would go to England while Lepinsky
  would proceed to Poland.
There were problems with connections
  then Lepinsky's wife got ill

but they decided Lepinsky should continue on
  as his tickets were non-refundable.
So when Lepinsky arrived in his hometown
  he was not in a good mood;
he'd had more hassles and worries
  than any old man should.

But now he was where most able-bodied men
  are in uniforms of some kind
and better fun than hassling old men
  rarely can they find.
There are men in green uniforms, blue uniforms, beige
  uniforms
  and uniforms of grey;
soldiers, and officers, police, customs men,
  militia men of various grades.
And there are secret police with identification tags
  and secret police without.
It takes a lot more coloured cloth to keep order
  than one would have thought.

There isn't much to this village: just
  the railway station and a store—
but order must be kept even in a place
  so small and poor.
So immediately Lepinsky steps off the train,
  a man in uniform demands
Lepinsky's papers, name, business, destination,
  social insurance number and his next of kin,
which reminds Lepinsky of his poor sick wife but
  Lepinsky does forebear
and gives the information and shows his papers
  albeit with a surly air.

Then Lepinsky starts walking through the village;
  on either side

of the dusty road are houses, with the land
  stretching out behind.
On each strip, there's one or more old women
  working on the land
with hoes; the old women are wrinkled
  and bony and bent.
I really hate to tell you
  but this I can't disguise;
women and hoes are the mode of production
  in the socialist paradise.

Lepinsky, of course, had seen it all before.
  However, I must mention
due to his bad mood, to quickly proceed to the house
  he was visiting was his intention.
But as he left the train station
  another uniformed gentleman
his papers, business, passport, and customs certificate
  did demand.
Lepinsky was even less pleased
  than before;
He'd been examined a lot and did not wish
  to be examined any more.

Still, as a peaceful man, albeit not one in a good mood,
  he did produce again
his papers, permits and permissions
  and his business he explained.
He then proceeded down the road and
  almost made it when a car
carrying four strong men with necks like bulls drove up
  beside this old man from Castlegar.
The women dug the fields with hoes because
  they had no machines
but strong men drove in cars
  and kept their hands clean.

Lepinsky thought they were parasites
  and Lepinsky told them so.
Lepinsky pointed at the fields and told the men they lived
  off the backs of those women with hoes.
Lepinsky spat on them, Lepinsky spat on their car,
  and he spat on their uniforms, Lepinsky did.
I don't know how he could move so fast
  but he ran to the house and hid.
He ran much faster than an old man
  from anywhere ought to,
having found himself in more trouble
  than he had sought to.

The house was surrounded by many men
  in different coloured cloth.
There were green uniforms, blue uniforms, beige
  uniforms,
    grey uniforms and uniforms of buff.
There were secret police with identification tags and there
  were secret police without identification tags.
That's where bad moods get you;
  Lepinsky had even lost his bags.
In alarm, he shouted through the window
  that he wasn't just any old man;
he was from Castlegar, owner of several hundred
  acres of land.

That cut no ice so now Lepinsky
  was so bothered
he had to say the chief of the secret police in Warsaw
  was his brother.
As he expected, all the huffle
  and kafuffle quieted down
although the men with guns and uniforms
  remained all around.

If the poor and dusty villagers
  weren't sufficiently amazed
they were due for more events that would
  leave them in a daze.

After a few hours, a STOL plane landed
  on the road beside the house;
the old women with no machinery to work the land,
  dropped their hoes
and fled into hiding. Then to his amazement,
  Lepinsky saw
step from the plane the chief
  of secret police in Warsaw.
Lepinsky unbarricaded himself and went outside
  to greet his brother
who, however, proceeded to curse the fact
  they had a common father.

The brother ordered Lepinsky to get in
  the plane and then ordered
the plane to fly back to Warsaw where he told
  his bad-tempered brother
you have three hours to leave Warsaw on the first plane out,
  no matter where it lands
and you will never again return to your home village
  or anywhere in Poland.
The old women went back to tilling
  the land with hoes.
and what they thought about it all,
  nobody knows.

Lepinsky didn't ask what would happen
  if he didn't leave there;
He went to the airport and caught
  the next plane to anywhere.

Just another old man dreaming of visiting home
   should be the end of this story
but predictability is not the way
   of history.
Any day now another crazy city person
   will buy four acres of land
and Lepinskys will be on their way to visit
   their respective homelands again.

THE DROOPING ROSE

Enough of the hugs and kisses already—
where's the romance?
Other men leave their families
so they can sing terribly sad but beautiful songs
of pain and longing
and have an excuse to drink themselves stupid.

And what about me?
Wouldn't I just once like to have
something to cry about other than money?
This drooping rose could be terribly symbolic,
instead, it's just got blackspot.
Blackspot!

Don't you read the books,
go to movies,
don't you even hear the songs on the radio?
Let's have romance—
you hiking down the road;
me weeping over a drooping rose.
Or me dying exotically.
(Women might outlive men but not in novels;
it's more romantic.)
You are now holding the drooping rose
and the sun is setting
or maybe the sun is rising
in dramatic contrast to your drooping rose.

Instead, we work together;
comfort each other over money and unemployment.
We laugh and play games
while the real world of pain and sorrow
passes us by.

Why don't you meet some other woman
you love nearly as much as me?
(Not as much as or you'll pay!)
It would be so dramatic with you having to choose
and me with the drooping rose.
Finally you decide you have to give her up
and now it's you with the drooping rose
with a single tear on its petals.

It would be so much more socially acceptable
than this never-ending harmony.
We'd have more friends then—
be really popular
and we'd understand how people could watch
modern movies without barfing;
get into watching TV without screaming.

How about you (or me) versus a career?
None of this looking for a job stuff.
Some men sacrifice their families to work.
And how come I never got to choose
between a husband and career
like all them women in middle class novels?
Just the other day I met a woman who told me
her fiancé wouldn't mind if she made more money.
At the time I merely wondered
how much garbage a human brain could hold.
But maybe that was romance?
It's either me or that boring awful job you hate.
It's either me or the garden.
It's either me or that baked halibut with lemon sauce.
Get rid of that mortgage or I'm gone.
It's either me or that drooping rose.

Enough of the hugging and kissing;
enough of the working together,
caring and sharing—
bring on the romance.

THE HERO OF 1981

So let's have 'em all run down the road
dying isn't pain enough
pain
we must have more pain
crying on the road to Thunder Bay
screaming down the road to Thunder Bay.

Dope pushers will make a killing on that road
exhorting pain-wracked bodies
to greater pain.

But will they cheer this motley crew in Thunder Bay?
I doubt they'll cheer this crew in Thunder Bay.

Running with one leg
is prettier
than making beds with one arm
typing with Hodgkin's Disease
teaching with Parkinson's
building trucks
with cancer of the spine.
Running is easier than working for a living.

There are no statues for those
who just worked all their lives
never making a spectacle of pain.
There is no glory in useful work.
No one cheers women who despite all odds
live.
No one cheers those who work their lives
in contribution to the society they are a part of.

Who has not known pain?
Who of us will not die one day?

Why is that only heroism on the part of
certain young white men?

There were crowds in Robson Square
thousands upon thousands
waiting for the dark so they could light their candles
waiting for the dark so they could light their candles
bring on the dark
so they can light their candles.

So here's to the eyeless, the faceless, the injured,
the cleaners, the cooks, the builders, the typists.
Here's to the angry, the bitter, the twisted.
Here's to the parents who cared for their kids.

THE LAST FEMINIST

What do you remember most?
Walking down Georgia.
Not betrayal; not defeat,
walking down Georgia.

What do you miss the most?
Walking down Georgia.
The days before
the ruling class could arrange
for us to see our liberation disappear
with the sisters rushing off
to join the middle class.
Walking down Georgia.

What do you hope for?
Not the goddesses they invented
to preach poverty to the poor;
wealth to the rich.
Walking down Georgia.

What do you fear the most?
Poverty and violence
and no more
walking down Georgia.

What did you think you were doing
walking down Georgia?
We were walking
for abortion;
for the right to control our own bodies.
For equal pay—
we thought women's work should be paid
the same as men's work.
For paid work—

we thought if a person did a job,
they should be paid for it.
For the right to organize
into groups of our own choice.
For the right to negotiate
about our own working conditions.
For day care
and all the raggle-taggle of children's rights.
(Children's rights are not important—
they're only a women's issue.)
Against sexism and racism and exploitation;
against poverty and violence and oppression.
For the right to jobs and promotion and pay
and to love whom we choose
and to live and laugh and raise children.
For safe houses and safe jobs
and streets where you don't die.
Hey, we dreamed of safe houses
and safe jobs and safe streets,
walking down Georgia.
(Dreams drown in blood.)

What do you dream about now?
Women and children
in our hundreds
in our thousands
walking down Georgia;
chanting and singing down Georgia;
yelling on Georgia;
carrying babies and balloons
and banners,
walking down Georgia.

THE QUESTION OF AUDIENCE

Audience is about ten metres wide
and about as long.
Sometimes it laughs;
sometimes it just stares at you
with its multiple paired eyes.
Audience hardly ever falls asleep
although parts of it may yawn.
An audience has many feet.
If you ask it a question,
it will not answer
but will shuffle some of its many feet.

THERE ARE PEOPLE

There are people in the city who have never had a home;
the streets of want and cold are all they know.
They sleep shivering in doorways or underneath a bridge,
while developers grow rich from human sorrow.

There are people in the city who have never had a job
that paid enough for clothing, food and rent;
while rich men and politicians pontificate and flaunt
the wealth that can be made from human sorrow.

The numbers of the homeless grow with every passing day
as high-priced condos and cement pollute the air
and poor people looking out from under bridges of despair
can see developers grow rich from human sorrow.

THE ROAD

Can somebody tell me what road I'm on?
I seem to be driving forever.
I don't recall starting and I can't see an end;
I just seem to be driving forever.

I'm sure I've been on this same road before—
the scenery all looks familiar.
I've driven along some roads in my time—
maybe all roads now look familiar.

There's a train track there over the river.
I've been on some trains in my time.
I've ridden some miles on buses,
and I've seen many roads in my time.

I don't know where I'm going, I don't know where I've
  been;
I can't raise a radio station.
There's just me in the car driving down this road
like the many I've seen in my time.

I've missed all the signposts that said where I've been,
I've not seen a town all these miles.
The trees by the road look like all other trees,
and I've seen many such roads in my time.

Can somebody tell me what road I'm on?
I seem to be driving forever.
I don't know where I'm going, I don't know where I've
  been,
I just seem to be driving forever.

The Rules Nowadays

The rules nowadays are:
we all must be thin,
white, or as near as we can get,
young, positive,
be able to cope with stress,
never get sick (illness is evidence of sin),
remember that anyone can get a job
if they really want to,
except that *we* don't get jobs,
we have careers,
and we must always make sure men wear condoms.

We should go around saying unions aren't necessary
as unions become even more necessary;
say unions are greedy
as wages drop;
unions have too much power,
as they lose what little power they had.

We must always be positive
and never be unhappy
except about refugees
swarming into our white culture in ones and twos;
never whine except about non-white immigrants,
unless they happen to win a gold medal
for Canada in the Olympics.

We must never say we're tired.
"Tired" doesn't exist any more.
If women got tired, they would have to rest
and if women rested,
the economy would collapse.
Since "tired" no longer exists,
it is named "illness" or "uncoped stress"

which is to be treated
with group therapy and aerobics
which make people so tired
hospitalization and/or drugs are necessary.
Drugs increase the GNP
whereas laying on the couch does not.

We ought to be kind to the worthy poor
at Christmas.
We must strive for sexual liberation
while children are sold as commodities on street corners.
We should remember that a woman's place is
in the home, in the factory, in the office,
in managerial positions, and in parliament,
all at the same time
and if they can't do that and raise their children
and reform the world
so children aren't sold on streets any more,
they are either sick (sinful)
or unable to cope with stress.

THE UNKNOWN CHILD
(from Frederic Wertham)

You have all heard praise of war—
for God and Country we send forth
killing men and killing machines
and afterwards build monuments
to battlefields, to generals,
to the unknown soldier.

Let us now build a monument
to the unknown child:
the one who died of hunger,
of war,
of epidemic disease,
of poverty,
of massacres,
died because it was born to parents
living in Tigre, Nicaragua, Haiti,
Chad, Lebanon, Palestine, Afghanistan
or some other obscure and war-torn,
poverty-stricken nation
The wise child knows to be born
to rich white parents;
the unwise choose the Amazon regions,
choose to be Bushmen
or Aborigines.

Let us now praise children
and build for them monuments.
Perhaps while building monuments,
we will remember the natural order—
that the older die before the younger;
that the younger must be nurtured
so they can grow and strengthen

and maybe some of them will know
some day
a way to live
without war and famine.

THOUGHTS WHILE PROOFREADING

You write the goddamn things
and then you gotta read 'em.
After you've proofread the manuscript,
you have to read it again
aloud at the launching.
Then you gotta read it again
and again and again and again
at readings and conferences.

Not only that, the conferences
have to be sat through.
Every conference has its own buzz words.
You learn one set and then at the next,
no one ever heard of "empower" or "deconstruct,"
they're into "insights," "holistic"
"sustaining" and
"don't lose your program."

I don't have time to write any more.
All I ever do is go to work
and come home, go to work, and come home,
except when I go to do a reading.
And my boss says
before I can become rich and famous
I have to give two weeks' notice.

TRANSPLANTS

Dying of illness in old age
is wasteful, is useless.
Slow dying destroys kidneys
wastes heart muscle
wears out liver.
Dying alone is sheer waste;
there has to be a doctor around
to rip out innards of the newly dead.

Organ donors have to die young,
die healthy,
die fast,
but not before they get to the hospital.

Be an organ donor:
drive too fast on a motorcycle.
Driving too fast, drunk, without a helmet,
is the doctor's ideal
as long as you don't die
until you get to the hospital.

Be an organ donor: kill.
Suicides and murders,
nice, gory murders,
lots of blood and guts and anguished screaming
of young folk dying healthy
dying slow enough to reach the hospital
but fast enough to preserve
those healthy young tissues.

It won't do for babies, though.
For a baby to be saved
another baby has to die.

Of course, we could always
kill the poor
so that the rich might live.
Be an organ donor:
join the poor of Calcutta.

Anything but old age.
Dirty old people
using up hearts and lungs and livers,
dying without any usable parts left:
saved from the benefits
of medical science,
saved from the cannibals.

UNCONSCIOUS

I'm going to write this poem, eh,
about this woman, who on the surface
looks really miserable,
but inside she's happy.
She's in this relationship, eh,
which looks bad, real bad,
but subconsciously is a warm, sharing,
deeply satisfying relationship
for both partners
although, of course, they don't realize it.
The children appear to be sodden lumps
but unconsciously they are well-adjusted
with a strong ego
and a good sense of identity.

They all end badly, of course,
because they don't know
that unconsciously,
they're in great shape.

That's a joke!
Who ever heard of uplifting urges
emanating from the unconscious?
It would put shrinks out of work.
Muck, not joy, is supposed to permeate
one's unfelt parts.

All you people out there—
you don't know how you really feel
or what you think,
until you pay some shrink to tell you
that inside you're a dangerous mess.
If they told you you were unconsciously
blissful and/or serene,

you would just sit around blissfully
and/or serenely
and not go back for high-priced appointments.
So you have to believe that your unconscious
is icky, disgusting poo.
Between your mucky innards
and your miserable rotten childhoods
you are a hopelessly gloomy
make-work project.
You don't even know what you think
about your therapist
unless the therapist tells you.

They know.
They say they know.
They swear they know.
They write treatises about it;
they get grants to research it;
they make you pay
before they will condescend
to inform you of it.
And you're so torn up about your childhood
you can't get up the nerve to tell them
it's a pile of crap
designed to make the rich richer
and the poor poorer.

So I'll tell you for free
that your unconscious is unconscious.
No murky muck
or mucky murk.
Don't you feel better already?

WAR AND POVERTY

War and poverty
are part of the same machine:
one kills
as surely as the other
and peace for the doomed children
of starvation
is just another word for dying.

WRITER'S BLOCK

Everybody knows about writer's block:
what you do for it is go
to a hotel room in Paris
or an isolated cabin in the Adirondacks,
if you can pronounce it,
with your portable typewriter
as it used to be;
now, of course, what you take along
is your laptop computer.

My boss had lawyer's block
most of June and
all of July.
One of her appointments one day
was a client preparing for
Examinations for Discovery.
It turned out this client
had client's block!
You can imagine
how that Discovery went!
They went to a hotel room in Paris
taking both the Petitioner's and Respondent's
List of Documents.

I miss my husband these days.
He was painting the front steps
and halfway through—
painter's block!
It was devastating.
He took his colour charts
and a book of wallpaper samples
and went to a hotel room in Paris.

Since he's gone,
I have to do my own shopping.
So I'm standing in the supermarket
checkout lineup the other day,
and my feet hurt and my head aches
and just as it gets to be my turn,
wouldn't you know it!
Cashier's block!

That hotel in Paris is getting full by now.
The rest of you better
learn how to pronounce
Adirondacks.

Coming Home

The pilot speaks with hesitation
and it appears he doesn't know
where we're going
or how long it will take to get there.
But the passengers have more faith
in pilots than politicians
and trust he will find the schedule
in due course.
And in the meantime,
I am dizzy from too many towns,
too many impressions,
grateful to too many people
whose names I will never remember,
who nourished me with songs
and sent me away with gifts.

I am going home to the husband I love
to take up our lives of quiet gratitude
for that which we have received;
for that with which we have not been afflicted.
The goddess has been kind
and if she has so chosen,
who am I to presume
that I am unworthy.